This book is dedicated to the writers group at Warwick.

Without their support and encouragement these words would not have been written.

60 Eclectic Poems for a Windy Day

by Wynn D. Day

Contents

HALLOWEEN

I'd felt a little queer – in this atmosphere,
But realised it was merely Halloween.
The streets felt deeply creepy
As I made my way home
In the dark. But hark!
A dog was barking.
I made my way quicker
And my torch began to flicker –
As across the church's path
I hastened on my way.

At first I heard a thud so low,
I felt around for somewhere to go
To hide from an advancing foe-
As surely it started closing in.

And there I waited – breathing baited
As behind a tombstone I took my rest.
The noise grew stronger,
And before much longer,
I saw a gang of skeletons
Come my way.

Banging drums, clashing cymbals
Passing quickly – oh so nimble;
Clattering, battering –
Not mattering anything
To these ghoulish shapes
Who hurried past my astonished gaze.

Their numbers grew
And a slew of them
Began to pound the ground
Began a knock, knock, knocking
On the graves.
Then witches and warlocks
Flew and grew into their numbers.

And as I felt my trembling soul,
I heard a clock begin to toll
Its midnight hour.

A swirl of smoke changed to a cloak
Which wrapped the babel tight.
It floated off into the night.

And I was left – the noise receding,
My head was spinning, the air was bleeding
In the silence and the mist.

LOUSY

We'll get the bitch to make her itch,
That's what we want to do.
To be infestin' we'll be nestin',
We stick to hair like glue.

You call us nits, we think you're twits,
You haven't got a clue.
When we invade and eggs are laid,
Our numbers soon accrue.

We creep and crawl and we're so small
You never know we're there.
And then we wait and proliferate
Till we've invaded all your hair.

And then you come to clear the scum.
To make us more accessible,
You try the comb and then the foam
But we're irrepressible!

So there you stand and spread your hands
And think what can be done.
To take the test and clear the pest
You think you'll have some fun.

Now you don't care, cause you despair,
And to clear the parasite,
You then decide – no place to hide
The scissors you indict.

Then snip snip snip and clip clip clip
Her hair falls to the floor,
With screams and blows the girl then knows
Her lovely hair's no more.

Well fancy that, the girl with the hat
Waits for her hair to grow.
With her bald head, she thinks we're dead –
But we'll be back you know…

ECCLISIA

Once upon a midnight clear
With icy air atremblin',
It seems the world was shot with fear,
When they find the ghouls assemblin'.

And there within the frigid air
An ochre eye of a killer.
Is staring madly; meant to scare
Like in Michael Jacksons 'Thriller'.

And sticky creatures flit about
In this land of degradation.
You sometimes hear the leader shout
As he cries in fulmination.

"I need a heavy man to chew
One that is sacerdotal.
Nothing less than this will do.
My appetite is total."

He summoned up a servitor
To do his ghastly bidding,
And with his slimy skin aglitter
Across the room came skidding.

"How can I please your lordship?"
Asked the lowly minion.
"Fetch the fast one with the horsewhip
To work in my dominion."

The one with the whip was Bustard
With a face shaped like a marrow.
And he was keen as mustard –
He charged round like an arrow.

"Yes, yes my liege. I'll fetch one now
I know just where to find him.
A slender one – if you'll allow,
The fat ones – they have pips in!"

So Bustard started on his quest
To find a slim presbyter.
He brought a monk for his master's fest
Struggling away – he was a fighter.

"I will not let you take a bite
Of my flesh so tasty,
I have a jealous catamite
Rambo, so don't be hasty."

The leader gave a look askance,
Who was this whipper snapper?
Would he be willing to take a chance
And be a brave kidnapper?

"I want someone – he is a dope,
I think you may know who.
He's also well known as the Pope
And no one else will do."

"I want to taste his tubby flesh.
I want to kiss his ring.
I want him back here nice and fresh.
I want to be the king!"

No one could do this grisly work
To try and get the pontiff.
The lead will have to go berserk –
Now we must stop this mischief.

I've written lots of nonsense,
I've nowhere else to go.
But now I say in my own defence
I think it's a real naff show!

THISTLES

We're down from bonny Scotland,
To this wheat field we were blown,
Packed in our Scottish parachutes
With the wheat seeds we were sown.

We stick our spiky purple heads
Above the parapet of wheat,
We like these rolling open fields,
But cannot stand the heat.

In Scotland we seek out the moors,
And live among the mists.
But now we're down here in this field
And our whole life now consists

To blow our clans around the field
With orders from our chief,
To spread our members far and wide
And cause the farmer grief.

And when it's time for ploughing,
Our seeds go in the mix,
Along with malted barley,
To the whisky for the fix.

So here's to all you connaisseurs,
Who drink the finest malt.
You think your scotch is pure as pure
But your taste buds we assault.

THE VULTURE

I hurried, worried to my house,
And glanced up to the sky,
And there I saw a large dark bird
Hov'ring round up high.

My thoughts about this harbinger
Were dismissive to say the least,
But my worried mind was weighted
With my thoughts about my beast.

How could I shift the thoughts of doom
That swam around my head?
Indeed so bad had it become
I often wished myself dead.

I looked up, and through my window
I saw the bird up close.
It seemed to me that the look
Upon his face was quite morose.

I chided myself, "How can a bird
Possess a look, a feeling, so profound?"
But when I opened up my door
He was perched upon the ground.

"You must not think," he said to me
"That all I do is fly.
I know the problems in your head
And I have a way for you to try

To rid yourself of all your grief,
If you will listen well.
The both of us can make a plan
To cease your journeying to hell.

I understand about the knife,
And the temper you displayed.
I saw the body lying there –
No wonder you're dismayed!

But you left your prints and many clues
For the authorities to find.
No wonder trouble weaves through your head
And you've so much on your mind."

"I think for you, the time has come,"
He said with no remorse,
"To turn the knife upon yourself
And I can help of course!"

I looked with utter disbelief
Into his face as he spoke.
I took the bird into my hands
And squeezed his neck till it broke.

And now I hear them at my door
A relentless nagging knock.
And I feel their rough hands beating me
As they throw me in the dock.

But then I wake with a heavy start,
And I look into the sky.
And watch in total wonderment
As a vulture passes by…

TWO SERPENTS

Two serpents sit down for tea
And gossip.
Their malevolent focus
Upon their absent friend
Who has provided the hostelry.
They whisper hissing secrets
And tell tales of gore.
They spit poison and drink poison
And quench their thirst
Whilst blackening her reputation.
The charlatans grow closer
Till their coils
Wind about the other,
Softly squeezing odium
For her demise.
They envenom and execrate
The very air they breathe
Until this toxic heap of coils
Morphs into pure, dripping poison.

SONG OF THE STINGER

I'm in a bag of rubbish
But I don't care,
I stick my head above the parapet
To see what's out there.
Cause I'm a stingy stinger
With nothing left to lose,
You dug me from my cosy bed
So did you hear the news?
I really am a hard nut,
Quite difficult to kill.
My very favourite pastime
That gives me such a thrill-
I like you to come close to me,
To give your flesh a stroke.
I love to see you jump away
As your anger you invoke.
However much you bash me down
I promise to come back,
Cause stingers are invincible,
A real hard nut to crack!

THE PIG STY

I have got a lovely farm,
It's the place I call my home.
And I have got a pig sty
So I am not alone.

So you could say I'm not alone
With the pig sty in my yard,
But I'm afraid to tell you
The incumbents make life hard.

So now you see my life is hard
'Cause those blighters make it so.
They infiltrate my every move;
They disturb my life's smooth flow.

They wreak havoc with my life's smooth flow
-It's a secret you must keep –
'Cause the sty is full of monsters,
And creatures from the deep.

The things these creatures from the deep
Inflict upon my mind –
The beat me up by day and night,
I think they're most unkind.

Well, I told you they are most unkind,
They attack me when I dream.
I wake up in a cold, cold sweat –
They always make me scream.

And when I wake up with a scream,
The day time's hard to bear.
I go off to the pig sty
And find there's nothing there.

And when I find there's nothing there
It makes me so upset.
I find I'm short of company
And then I start to fret...

The feelings when I start to fret
Grow bigger day by day.
I search for something all the time –
I have got to find a way.

I really have to find a way
To help my mind to clear.
I just can't seem to do it,
It's the very thing I fear.

And so this deep and lonely fear
I think is here to stay.
I wish that I could find a cure
For the demons to fade away.

And if my demons fade away,
What a lovely life I'd live.
My days and nights just sweetness;
Oh, Jesus what I'd give.

Oh, Jesus; all the world I'd give
To have never done that deed,
When I took the knife and hacked and chopped
And left the man to bleed.

And I watched him writhe and bleed and bleed
As he lay upon the ground.
The wind was still, the night was dark,
There was not a single sound.

Upon that night there was no sound,
As I laid him in his grave.
He lies beneath the pigsty,
But his company I crave.

But the company so much I crave
Does me not a bit of good.
I have demons now instead of him
And now here's a man with scythe and hood.

Here stands the man with scythe and hood,
To take me on my way.
Thank God he's come to fetch me now
To take me where he may…

GRACE'S AIR

In a high corner, in a space,
Sits a lady- tall, with grace.
Busy looking for a place to dwell,
She thinks, "This place will do me well,
I can make it cosy and good
And it's just right for motherhood."

She works away and weaves and hooks
Pendulous gossamers, and looks
With satisfaction and with pride.
She quickly lines her nook to hide
Her dots. Imperceptible, black.
They hang suspended at her back.

Around the dots in miniature time
Appear eight tiny hairs, very fine,
Which slowly turn blacker, longer;
Gently, quickly they grow stronger,
Savouring their protective mother,
As she stands guard before the brothers.

Their time has come, she's ceased her giving,
And with long legs to procure a living
They disappear – the long legged dots.
Now the tall and elegant lady knots
Her web, and continues to hang and spin
As her offspring fade deep into oblivion.

THREE GIFTS

How do I show my affection for her?
A red rose?
No, not my style.
Chocolate?
No, she's too fat.
But here –
From the fruits of my labour –
A putty duck,
With a thick neck
And a bill too big.
A putty dice
Having only one numbered face,
Showing a trey –
The three prongs of my fork.
And a putty poached egg,
Baptized with orange juice –
For a yoke.

SURFERS LAMENT

Each morning when I wake up
In my cozy bed,
I reach for my computer
-it's right there by my head.

It's just where I left it,
Before I went to sleep,
So now I turn it on once more
To the programs where I keep

My facebook, twitter and Instagram,
Where I'm buzzing once again.
There's so much here
To get me high and stimulate my brain.

I could stay here forever,
Just chatting to my friends,
But I have to get and start the day
Though I have messages to send.

I'm off and walking down the street
Making sure I'm fully wired,
There's a pic of someone's breakfast
When I'm looking to be inspired!

But never mind, it won't take long
I'm going to change my search.
There's someone in Mongolia
And something about a church.

There's someone being murdered!
Oh, what am I to do?
Oh, look it's only Youtube,
What a shock! I thought it was true.

So busy, busy all day long
I move the cursor round.
I'm so immersed in all my biz
I never make a sound.

Time hurries past to evening tide,
And now I realise,
I haven't spoken to a soul
But I'm feeling very wise.

I've been connected to the world,
But now the day is done,
I need to call up Google
For bedroom story fun.

There really isn't any time
To spare all through the day,
To seek out human company
On my pc I must play.

But sometimes I get feelings
When I think there's something wrong,
When loneliness will hit me
And for loving arms I long.

I seem to get psychotic
When my mind runs on ahead,
And often I get feelings
When I wish that I was dead.

The genie's out the bottle
For this madness I pursue.
I've found this is all I know
There's nothing else to do.

I see my life just stretching out
Being wired to this machine
Just like a drug – I'm hooked
And I never will get clean.

A FINAL KISS

Upon the murmurs of the night,
I think I hear an angel call.
I start, and listen as I might
To hear the undulations in the pall
Of darkness. As beside me lays
A man I had but lately ushered in.
Along lewd pathways we had strayed.
But now his breath is growing thin.
I know – I feel a presence there –
A spectre? Who knows? But as I cry
With fear so great, I say a prayer –
His body tightens as he dies.
I feel him draw his last breath –
He has had the kiss of death.

THE PRAYER AND THE SERPENT

Through the lych gate to the house of God
The sinner stands heavy with guilt.
He fears the worst, fears for his blood-
For the house of cards he built.
The altar carpet accepts his kneel
And with meek supplication
Tells the lord how he feels.
A soulmate slithers for his oration,
With its green and evil eye,
It hears the sinner ask to be forgiven,
And now his crimes it will pry.
All forgiveness now is riven.
Its coils twist round his limbs
Chance for God's redemption dims.

IN MY WILDEST DREAMS

In my wildest dreams,
I wrestled with old lovers
In a timeless tunnel,
Within turbulent grey clouds,
Undulating to the rhythms
Of bygone days.

I saw their eyes fix mine,
I felt the rapture suffuse me,
Across the winds of time.
I hear their voices –
Calling, calling me to come

Return with them,
Sink in a whirlpool once again
Of eclectic esperance.
Oh how each echo races with me on raging wind.
Remember. please remember me.

In my wildest dreams
I reach out to them.
But like their passing
The image passes
Just out of reach.
And the cold night wind
Takes them back to the deep.

THE GAME OF CARDS

They played upon a richly coloured tapestry tapis.
The silent, strong, subtle sort
Who never countenanced defeat,
And a young woman,
Confident and happy with her game.
She gazed at her cards
And considered deep her options.
Her fingers wondered along
The face of the faces
With expressions inscrutable and unbending.
Which card should she choose?
In her flamboyant naivety
She took a queen
And proudly boasted her reflected regality
To her opponent.
He waited.
A four, a seven, a two.
Nonchalantly, insignificant
Cards followed one upon another.
Then the game plan altered.
Lines were drawn upon her face.
She found a mirror
And was horrified at their etchings
And her fingers followed their contours.
She found bundles of problems
Thrown at her feet.
She did not know what to do
Except she realised
She was still expected to continue
Her game of cards.
She perceived her opponents laughter
But heard none.
Still the cards were played.
Sometimes the game was easy;
Sometimes the sun would shine;
But it was relentless.
Sometimes there were dark moments
When she no longer cared to play,
But her opponent took away her choices

And she was forced to take
Perpetual nothingness
Or continue to struggle
With a mighty game
Which in turn surprised and appalled her.
The lines on her face
Deepened – filled up with cares,
And she realised her hand
No longer held any cards of influence.
And she quietly played them
Until they all ran out.

BATTLE DREAM

I dreamed of a battle
When God was killed.
He had been my whole life,
The Lord, My God.
I wanted to take Him
To bury Him
But others stole Him from me
And defamed me
For my neglect of Him.
They took Him, and buried Him
And soundly kicked me.
They forced me to regard their actions
And poured dull sloth upon me.
I was forced to retreat,
While they engaged
In their madness around me.
When all was quiet
The evil countenances looked around
And then they slunk away.
Finished.
But I was not finished.
The Lord my God was dead
And I was left to avenge Him.
I sat with Time and waited.
Soon the scene changed
And my silent battle commenced.
And I avenged my Lord.
And He was well pleased.

THE HANGING TOWER

His finely tuned eye
Homes in on the tower.
It's fetid vapour; it's evil attraction
Draws him.
He moves in closely
Feeling its fascination.
He sees its writhing deadly escalation
Of twitching legs;
Wings or heads stuck tight,
A stunted delivery of devilry.
Up and down
Its glossy surface
Stickily entombed compatriots
Lie stuck fast –
In their death throes or dead –
In their glorious adversity!
Can he resist its divine temptation?
Its glutinous resin?
Its come hither smell?
Intoxicated, he buzzes closer.
The sun glints on the hanging tower,
And it glitters with sticky.

THE TALE OF THE TICK (A true story of a foreign pest)

"Oh, la la la," said the tick
"This Gallic countryside
Makes me sick.
I think I fancy a foreign trip.
I'll find a host, and a sailing ship."

Where he lived wasn't too good,
It was in a cow's ear
Near to Menez Meur Wood.
As the cow moved he fell in the mud.
"I must find a dog and suck its' blood."

He waited patiently upon the floor
As time went by
It became a bore.
But soon young Ami came running by
"Ah, here is a dog – I'll give her a try!"

He jumped up very quickly
From off the ground
And thought how lucky 'cause he'd found
A dog of the highest pedigree,
Now his trip to England would be guaranteed.

"Oh, la la la," said the tick,
"This golden ear
Will do the trick."
He lodged himself upon her skin,
And wrapped himself round like a safety pin.

He nestled down in comfort there,
And hid himself
Beneath her hair.
And no one knew as he safely fed,
And he lay undetected in his cosy bed.

And soon Ami returned to Angleterre
And his passage
On the ship was then set fair.
But his idyll there would not last long
As at the vet they found something wrong.

"Oh, la la la," said the vet,
"I see a French tick
Upon your pet."
And with a device neat and small
She turned and turned for the ticks' withdrawal.

And then with a long sharp pin
She pierced deep
The poor ticks' skin.
And just as his end was nigh
For sure they heard his final cry.

"Oh, la la la," said the tick
"For sure for sure I sure am sick.
I wish I'd stayed in my beloved France.
At least on the cows
I'd have stood a chance."

A LOUD GUFFAW

In the madcap world of Frankie,
Upon his feet and legs so lanky
Sat a pair of shoes so swanky –
Made him think of hanky panky.

So then he called up his friend Lance
And asked him if he would perchance
Like to go to the town hall dance –
'Cause he knew of a girl called Nance

And if he could get her upon the floor,
He knew his charms she could not ignore.
"Let's go outside," she would implore.
Lance responded with a loud guffaw.

"Yeah, let's go and take the chance
To find ourselves a new romance."
So to the town hall they did prance,
And the burly bouncer at the entrance…

"You can't come here with shoes so swanky,
You pair of nerds so long and lanky.
Your sort come here for hanky panky,
So get off home now Lance and Frankie."

"But we've come down here to meet Nance.
We thought we might have half a chance
To get her on the floor to dance –
You know the way we guys advance!"

"You guys have come here just to score,
But all the girls think you're just a bore.
I just seen Nance and she swore
You touch her, and she'll get the law."

So open mouthed stood Frankie and Lance
When they knew they had no chance
To even get the smallest glance
Of the fair and lovely Nance!

So back to Lance's they did restore,
And on the way they priced a whore.
So all's not lost heretofore,
Now both of them pay for the score!

AN OFFER YOU CAN'T REFUSE

I see you stop to gaze at me.
I sense your breathlessness.
Do I steal your breath
Because my tangled vine
And bright red fruit
Attract your pallet?
Move closer.
See how my conflated tendrils
Entwine each other
To show the better
My sumptuous berries.
Come hither – come hither.
They're here for the taking.
This perfect vermillion
Compares with the brightest jewel.
Mine are also priceless.
Where will you see an exhibition
To match my delicious gratuity?
They are yours.
Feel their smooth textures
As they mingle your salivary juices,
And slide their way
To oblivious digestion.
You move away.
How can you resist an offer
From Eve's serpent?
Maybe your elevated sensibilities
Will send you to resist an
Alternative temptation?
But I think not.

TIDE

Sleeping sand
Feathered by creeping wavelets.
Frothy, burping bubbles
Disturb the damp repose
And sun- bleached surface,
To steal it back
And hide it
Under a mountain of water.

As the feathers gain strength
Chunky white surfed arms
Gather swathes of sand
Rudely wake it, cover it
Take it
Replace its space
With bobbing boats.
And sailors with nets and pots,
Who garner its sleeping crabs and lobsters.
They wake to the rush and gush
Of commanding sea
And the return of Neptune's knickerbockers!

THE HEADSTONE (for John)

He dropped his head and ceased to view the world.
The man whose life had meant so much to me.
But time would show the actions, now unfurled
That made our separation come to be.
From woodwork stock they clambered in,
His home and life – they sought to shut me out.
At his demise his little wife should win –
They'd show the world and there'd be no doubt.
Whatever words, now are set in stone,
The words that passed between us were the truth.
Hearts and minds entwined, but now alone
And so much love, I know, I have the proof.
How these headstones do deceive!
The truth of it – you would not believe…

COOKING MINDS WITH CANNABIS

A fluff of smoke
That hangs lazy grey threads on the air.
A gust of helpless laughter
Where it has played miasmic mind games
As it curled the chemistry
In the passages of thought
Of its victim.

The warm breeze has blown
Through the green slender fronds
To contort this madly, magical elixir,
And bestow gifts
Of a temporary happy heaven
Where every sinew rejoices
In its perfect relaxation.

But in its strands of ghostly mysticism,
An amorphosis is at work.
Quietly and unseen in the shadow
It lurks. Then one day
It endows with cachinnation, a vicious rictus;
Rigid, intransigent.
Its gnarled fancy
Corrupting and corrupted.
Bed mates with insanity.

NONSUCH

Once upon a midnight clear
With the icy air atremblin',
It seems the world was shot with fear,
Then they find the ghouls assemblin'.

And there within the frigid air
Dwell the ochre eyes of a killer.
Staring madly; meant to scare
Like in Michael Jacksons 'Thriller'.

And sticky creatures flit about
In this land of degradation.
You sometimes hear the leader shout
As he cries in fulmination.

"I need a heavy man to chew
One that is sacerdotal.
Nothing less than this will do.
My appetite is total."

He summoned up a servitor
To do his ghastly bidding
And with his slimy skin aglitter
Across the room came skidding.

"How can I please your lordship?"
Asked the lowly minion.
"Fetch the fast one with the horsewhip
To work in my dominion."

The one in charge was Bustard
With a face shaped like a marrow.
And he was keen as mustard –
He charged round like an arrow.

"Yes, yes my liege. I'll fetch one now
I know just where to find him.
A slender one – if you'll allow,
The fat one – they have pips in!"

So Bustard started on his quest
To find himself a presbyter.
He brought a monk for his master's fest
Always struggling – he was a fighter.

IN A HOLE

They're stiff. And dead. And lifeless.
Cold in their coffins.
But they linger on earth.
Not in it.
Waiting for the hours to pass –
To slip away –
So that the corpses box may feel the thud of earth.
But not yet.
Their hours on earth go on…
Though their clock has stopped.
And silence and stillness
Are their companions.
But the custodians of the dead
Talk and chatter
To the stillness in the box.
"You look lovely," they reassure
Reassure the rotting body in the box
Whom they pamper
And beautify
To make them feel special
To meet their maker
In a hole.

They ride in style
For once – important.
Sung about and prayed for
Till the thud, thud, thud –
And the person in the buried box
Rots perdurably.

THEN

House of expectations
Waiting for the ghosts
Of past pleasures
To return.
Sensing their echoes
In the bleak landscape
Of present time.
Shadows of those
Who once walked there.
Laughter.
Music.
How to let go?
How to watch memories
Like ships, sailing away –
Away
Never to return.
How to turn your back
And walk away
Haunted.
Stalked by shadows
Who beckon and mock
"Never let go, never let go."
But the ship has left
And dumped its cargo
Of memories,
Which cling and curse
As you try to leave.
"Don't go. Don't give us away.
This was once you.
By leaving, you leave
Part of yourself."

IN CELEBRATION OF LOVE

Ah, the panache of falling in love!
Tumbling into a vat of churning chemicals.
Swirling, steamy passions
Emanating from every cranny in the body.
Needy; where is he?
Swooning glances and
Ponderous sighs –
Where is he, where is he?
Ahhh.
Swimming, sinking.

In an incantation of esperance.
Lying on a rocky shore
Soft waves caressing
This love, this love, this love.
A dewy eyed monster
Sends out gentle gossamer threads
To tangle tight,
And gently bond every inner freedom,
Till the whole sticky world
Circles this object of love!

QUIETUS FOR THE FAIRY

I first saw her in a hollow spotlight,
Drowning.
An outcast cast out from Titania's palace.
Hurt and grey.
Her demeanor sore
Tortile.
Her delicate filigree wings
Crumpled.
An unseen mortal wound.
As the piercing shape of light
Denudated her wings
She sank down to die
From her lacy existence.
Like a sad butterfly
Whose damaged pinions
Flake like desiccated paper.
Silently her strength melted
As she drew her last breath,
And the tiny cursed skeleton
Luxated to star dust.

OFF TO HELL?

He stole the soul that once was mine
As I had crossed a dark parapet
So now he drank deep of the poisoned wine.
I'd had him to my house to dine
And talked to him about the debt.
He'd stole the soul that once was mine.
He sifted through my jewels so fine
His evil talk pulled me into his net
And now he drank deep of the poisoned wine.
So sure was I of his fast decline,
And with panicked eyes he began to sweat.
He stole the soul that once was mine.
As death drew near he gave a sign
So sure was I that his breath must cease, and yet
Still he drank deep of the poisoned wine!
Then I paced the floor and waited for the time
When Beelzebub his corpse would get.
He stole the soul that once was mine,
And he had drank deep of the poisoned wine.

FOOTSTEPS

I hear the footsteps
Out there.
They seem to be approaching
But come no nearer.
They are there.
It may be ghostly soldiers
Sightless, directionless, lifeless.
But advancing. Relentless.
So I seek a hiding place,
But the footsteps continue.
The beat, beat, beat
But as I look there is nothing.
No one.
Not even a mist
Just the beat of footsteps.
I listen for music
But hear only footsteps.
Like a dark heart
The beat of the approach
Becomes the music
Of relentless footsteps coming…

THE COWS AND PIES

Me and my friend, we went away,
And zoomed across the skies.
We went to stay with cotton face May
To learn how to bake some pies.

But first we had to kill the cows
Before they ran away,
May got her gun to show us how
To shoot them through the hay.

But her cows were very wise,
And knew her little ploys.
She'd have to wait to get her prize
Cause they'd make lots of noise.

They boomed and bellowed across the field,
And made the neighbours think
These cows their milk they would not yield-
No milk for them to drink.

So one brave neighbour sidled up
And said, "Hey, what's the game?
I'll have no milk inside my cup
And you're the one I'll blame."

Exasperated, May got mad.
"Now, just you bugger off.
There's no more milk here to be had.
Go! Or you're in the trough!"

But then the neighbour took her gun
And pushed old May aside.
My friend and I began to run
To find somewhere to hide.

Inside the silo tall and brave,
We hid behind the door.
Outside we heard May rant and rave,
Then she crawled round on the floor.

"Now look here May we only came
To learn to cook some pies.
Instead it seems that you're insane
And also full of lies."

And then the neighbour stumbled in
Still looking for a fight.
My friend and I jumped in the bin
And left May to her plight.

The gun went bang and up May sprang
And got him by the throat.
And as we watched in came a gang
Of whiskered billy goats!

And butt, butt, butt, they butted bums
And threw them to the floor.
Then what a surprise in there comes
Officers of the law!

"Now what's all this?" they shouted out.
Horrified May looked on.
"We have to know what it's all about
And where the shots came from."

"It wasn't me." And then she said,
"They started all the noise."
The neighbour held his throat and head
Then pointed to us boys.

"Them two there made all this trouble."
Then we jumped out of the bin.
And across the fields on the double
Pondering on our sin.

Well stuff the pies and stuff the cows
We'll make our way back home.
We don't need May to teach us how
To never need to roam!

YESTERDAY

Yesterday, I found my way to the sea.
Me and dogs.
The waves crashed and smashed
As they dashed to the shore.
We eyed the foam, white honeycomb.
Monochrome waves.
Nature's slaves,
And also the graves of men who bravely
Sailed this ocean.
Their cries can't be heard,
And never a word is spoken
In hushed reverence,
In the voices of yesterday.

THE SPRITE CHILD

A shadow looked on from Pew Tor.
For a child was lost that night.
The pixies danced round ever more.
A young girl searched and then saw
A figure moving in the moonlight.
A shadow looked on from Pew Tor,
She hurried on and then saw
A jig, a pirouette, a sprite!
And pixies danced round ever more.
Oreads and cobald with claw
They held their revels in her sight.
While a shadow looked on from Pew Tor.
She looked across to the windlestraw
And there was the child as their acolyte.
The pixies dance round ever more.
He swayed with the group in the haw
And his smile shone with pure delight.
A shadow looked on from Pew Tor,
And pixies danced round ever more.

WITHOUT YOU

Truth and death walk hand in hand
Just as death is leaving.
They meet as brothers – yet understand
A tragic spell they're weaving.

Before the salty tears have dried,
Truth meets up face to face
With reality, and for those who cried
Anger, denial and loss to embrace.

And lots of questions, "Why, oh why
Did they have to leave this way?
If they had stayed, then we could try
To have said all we had to say."

Unspoken words bring in regret
With the years that stretch ahead.
And time that runs so fast with them, yet
They don't want to be with their dead.

And then when truth has finally shown,
What they always really knew.
That now they are quite alone –
Life goes on within you and without you.

THE BALLAD OF HALL SANDS

They stole our sand and beach away
To make a smart new dock.
They took away our livelihoods
When we lived beneath the rock.

Our menfolk fished the local sea,
And so our village thrived.
With grocers, bakers, pubs and all –
It was good to be alive.

John Jackson was the big man's name
Who made the dredging start.
He sent machines to steal the sand
To tear us all apart.

The village folk begged on their knees
Pleading with them to cease.
But they took their 60,000 tons
From then, there was no peace.

The storms of winter 1903
Swept in and crashed our homes.
From other storms we were not spared
The devastation of sea foam.

Salt water down the chimneys,
Doors and windows all caved in.
The careless men from Plymouth
Were the masters of this sin.

So now with coast eroded;
The village lost to time.
The unsafe coast path moved inland –
No cure for docklands crime.

BUSY WIND

What busy little grasses
When our windy uncle passes,
He sets us all running really wild.
We run so busy busy
He makes us fizzy fizzy
Faster now than any little child.

He's our wicked uncle Russell
Who makes all this hustle bustle,
And he turns the ocean waves very wild.
All the boats are topsy turvy
On the waves so very curvy,
But a busy wind will always make you smile!

THE ANGRY BANJO

We wanted to hear his ukulele,
But they said he's gone to his Bordello,
Then out he came with his shillelagh.
Someone said he'd been off with Hayley,
We thought that would have made him mellow.
We wanted to hear his ukulele,
We loved the rhythm played so gaily.
We also liked to hear his cello,
Then out he came with his shillelagh.
We said "He'll find himself at the Old Bailey
He really is a silly fellow."
We wanted to hear his ukulele
And get him to come with us to the ceilidh,
But then we thought we heard him bellow,
And out he came with his shillelagh.
We'd just wanted to hear him daily,
And go along just to say hello!
We wanted to hear his ukulele,
But out he came with his shillelagh.

THE ROOM

Come in, come in and welcome
There's room always for you here.
Bring with you all your memories
Of the sixties, of closeness, of beer.

All the folk who chatted and laughed long,
The talked and they groused and they smoked.
They were big, and they filled the room closely,
It hummed all with love as they joked.

Each one in this group was so special,
And this story – if all goes to plan,
Tells the tale of the people who laughed there,
And the one in the middle was my gran.

Her chair was right under the window,
-This of course was just second place –
But a reason for why it was put there
Was her callers could chat face to face.

Invariably, grandad would leave her,
As the horse racing beckoned most days.
After granny had dusted and dished up
Lunch, he'd be off, resolutely in his ways.

They were poor, and no phone was installed there,
So we went there her company to seek.
She was glad, she was good and was happy
If her room was full up every week.

With her children, their spouses and families,
When they got there they always would find
Conversation, good company and gossip,
And their problems - she never would mind.

As a child I would be there and listen,
As the stories abounded and grew.
I'd play cards, or I'd view postcard humour,
In this wonderland, time always flew.

But the people who gathered around me,
In that room full of love – so secure,
Most have left, gone away on a journey,
Somewhere else, somewhere better –I'm not sure.

And as each one has left they have taken,
A part of my life with them there.
I grew angrier as each one departed.
When they went, did they think I'd not care?

As the years have fled, I've reflected-
I'm in grief cause I miss them so much.
My dad, all my aunties and uncles
And my gran with her so special touch.

With her brand of good humour and gossip
How I long for those halcyon days!
When we chatted and giggled and spent time
Being together. What tricks mem'ry plays!

I know I shall spend my life longing
Just to see her sweet face once again.
And the reason for why I don't have her
P'raps, some day will all become plain?

ODE TO A PHOTO

There she sits
Full of rounded goodness,
Breathing bracing
Blackpool
In its mid-fifties bloom
   Of common decency
      Good behaviour
         And kiss me quick! Oooh!
Naughty slogans
For easy humour
And common camaraderie.
Joy for the world
From the lady
Brimming cheerfulness,
Who sits smiling benevolently
Effortlessly oozing love
For her people, for her life.

She's on her holidays
Beneath the concrete
Beneath the stained glass.
Posing for eternity
Posing for the love of us
Oozing her love
Which goes on, and on,
        and on
          and on…

AURORA's AWAKENING

She opens sleepy eyes.
"What, time for day so soon?"
But the hurrying shadows prod her.
"It's almost time for us to leave."
Her charcoal ringlets sweep across the sky
Opening chinks for clouds to float through.
A reluctant star resists her telling,
But an orangy moon slips sleepily towards his horizon bed.
"Come and join me, my beautiful star."
She blinks her eye – shut – and is fled.
The lazy lady shakes her curls once more,
Peppers more stars,
And breaths a large blue yawn of dawn
To open wide the door of heaven
For daylight to tumble aloft.
Thick and fast it dusts the disappearing night,
And the lazy lady with her spent curls
Sits up and views her pretty sleepy world filled with summer,
And through the cracks of her smile
Yet more light filters out.
"Mmm, 4am.
Good morning world,
I give you my early day
So you may dance with me in breathless delight."

ADIEU ODE

A windy night in summer,
Memories from Christmas's long ago
Curl to me on the cool breeze.

The comforting pleasure of
A social club full of those gathered
To celebrate the season of goodwill.
Music with a hissing snare.
Hissing singers at a microphone,
Many legs and bums
Moving to the boom-boom rhythm –
Santa is coming tonight!

I feel the presence of people long dead
Who loved and cared for me

The sound of the Beatles wanting to hold my hand.
The magic.
The sparkle and stardust –

Waiting yet, for today's little ones
Who will soon stand in wonder
As I did in those sixties Decembers.
Will they feel the same glow as me?

The same secure arms
To carry them to their beds,
To await the mystical coming of the day,
And awake to the excitement,
And caring people
Coming together as one
In joyous celebration.

Oh, to feel that love once more.
To see the faces full of kindness –
And to express that long ago adoration
To them.
Adieu, my people, adieu.

MEETING

I make my way through the mist
With the smuggler in pursuit.
I fear the blackness of the moor
And the thud of the buccaneers boot.

I stumble on into the gorge
And listen to my heartbeat.
A rapid drum in the still dark night…
And suddenly our eyes meet.

He takes me roughly by the throat
His breath is dank and stale.
"My pretty one," he says to me,
"I want my treasure. Do not fail

To tell me the secrets that you keep.
I know 'twas you who stole
Into my chamber upon that night-
Now give it back – I want the whole

Lot. And do not think," he roughly says,
As he shakes me to the bone.
"That I will let you get away…" A noise-
And I know we're not alone.

Where the waters meet and fall
A presence steps into our midst.
With horned head, and arrowed cane
A swish of the tail and a hiss…

"The treasure – that of which you speak
I'll have you know full well,
Belongs to me. Now hear me speak –
Return it to my hell.

The both of you shall know my wrath
If you dare to disobey."
And then to me, "Go fetch it quick
And by the light of day

You shall place it closely in my cove
By yonder waterfall.
And you," he says to my foe as he tosses him to the ground,
"Be gone." The buck, in fright, away begins to crawl,

But the blackened shape as he tries to escape
Is cast into the fires of hell.
His screams will haunt me, and his face
As into the furnace he fell.

I look to the eyes of Beelzebub.
"Now this shall be your fate
If by some chance my treasure you
Do not deliver. I warn you – don't be late!"

So now I race across the moor
With the devil in hot pursuit.
But how can I get the message across-
I have never had his loot!

VOICE FROM THE TOWPATH

Gary Glitter leading his gang
Medicine Head watching their rising sun
The apache war cry of 10cc
And the search for sweet gypsy Rose…

The strains follow me as I look across the towpath.
I see the burgeoning chestnuts
Growing in the same tree
That stood there all those years ago.
I see myself garnering burrs.
I hear the sound of my sister's laughter,
I smell the cool autumn breezes
The same ones that greeted me then.

As I look, I feel a gnarled hand
Extending across the water
Inviting me back.
"Step across my invisibility
And see what you lost.
Your innocent young features
Now furrowed with care,
And your mind crowded with life.
Step over here
And you may wear once more
The turquoise seersucker dress of that summer,
You may feel again the glorious days of youth.
Step back…step back…"

Ava May continues her silent sleep.

FROGS

Upon one night in March this year,
Two frisky frogs went courting.
They met beneath the moon so clear
Both eager to be snorting.

At the height of their assignation
They laid a sheen of eggs.
Then mighty pleased with their night's work
Hopped off upon their legs.

Off they went to slimy climes,
And left the spawn to bake there.
And through the warm and rainy times,
The black eggs thrived in balmy air.

Then as the wavelets lapped the bank,
The tiny babes were dropped.
Through jellied holes down they sank.
See there they go. Plop, plop, plopped.

The days go on. See how they grow,
They're turning into tadpoles!
Like giant sperms around they flow
All looking for their boltholes.

Then as they metamorphasize
And grow their little leglets,
They lift their faces, you hear their cries –
They're turning into froglets!

BEEWOCKY

The fowl and the cattypuss
Went to bee…
Down a beautiful bee-off slope.
They took some honey (for the bees)
And plenty of tissues in case they sneeze,
With bee stings all aloft.

The fowl looked up to the bees above
And sang a bee sting melody
To the bees buzzing in harmony.
"Oh, lovely bees, kiss kiss buzz kiss
Kiss buzz kiss kiss, oh bees!

Oh bees, all alive, let us make you a hive
To wax lyrical down in the bongs."

So off they went for the bees to bong.
And there on Queen Hill
Ambrosia rings of blossoms
Bonged to the bees.

Then the fowl and the cattypuss
Had a connubiality – and a turkey dinner
And danced to the buzz of the bees.

With thanks to Jim and Sacha for their contributions.

VIRUS

We're virulent! You're working hard
To get the numbers down.
You carelessly just go about
While we creep into town.

And there you are – all into love
Requiring a kiss.
You play so well into our hands
Our viral spikes can't miss.

We like the weak, we like the old,
They're our first strike.
But we are there to watch you all
Our aim is to hitchhike.

We change our ways to baffle you
But we know you are smart.
We like to see you dressed in black
As we rip your world apart.

As more and more of you succumb
When we have our wicked way.
Hospital beds fill up and up
As we multiply day by day.

Your lives have grown pathetic
As you've gone through the years.
This is nature's payback
To cause you many tears.

And on and on and on we go
Cause we have lots to gain.
African brothers are working well
To find a tougher strain.

Infect, infect, infect again
And stuff your vaccination.
And now we can raise a toast
And drink in a libation.

THE MUSHROOM HOLIDAY

The mushrooms lay inside their beds
All waiting for the morn,
When all the spores would yield their crop
And babies would be born.

And all could then be gathered in,
And shoved inside the van
So they could then be carted off,
And put inside a can.

But no, the time is finally here
To give these guys a break.
And use them not for fodder
But a seaside holiday to take.

With cases packed and sarnie's made,
They're off to their hotel.
Then on with shorts and tee shirts
To raise a little hell.

They're building lots of sandcastles
And hope to get a tan.
To show to all the ones at home
And prove that they can

Indulge themselves out in the sun
Without them getting soggy,
And be as fresh as new boys,
And not be feeling groggy.

But things did not go right
As their tee shirts start to stick,
And though their tan progresses well,
They're starting to feel sick.

The beach is full of mushrooms
Throwing up in all the places,
And if we look more closely,
They all have sticky faces.

The other folk upon the beach
All get a frying pan,
To throw the mushrooms in there
And catch them if they can.

And now for the beach barbeque
Everyone's invited!
And all the people gather round
While the stoves are all ignited.

The mushes are not having this
And jump up on their feet.
"We're not here to be eaten,
We've come down for a treat!"

But no one listens to them,
They're waiting for their tea,
Especially cause the mushrooms
Have been laid on all for free.

So they're sautéed, roasted, chopped
                              and stuffed
And go down very well.
So like Lewis Carroll's oysters
To the swindlers they fell.

MUSHROOMS

– chain verse

The mushrooms came up from the woods
They walked upon the sward. They jumped
To live inside the pie.

They live inside the pie, to avoid the pan.
They looked for their button bros,
And pulled them one by one.

And pulled them one by one. Inside the pie.
No more smelly garlic, sautee or risotto
Just chicken friends.

Just chicken friends. Around, about
To party with, get stuffed with and just to be
Chicken and mushroom pie!

PASSAGE

His cares doubled, his mind troubled
He lays his head down to die.
There is sighing and crying –
No spirit is flying –
It stays inside the dead.
The mourners walk
And talk sadly of their loss.
But his body lies in suspension
Entombed in tension
Is there no redemption here?

The night is dark,
The funeral clerk
Stops work for the day.
He puts away his things
And flings his jacket –
When sounds abound
From the body boxes next door.
Upon the floor
A shadow hastens into the night.
He sees the flight
And breathes.

A troubled spirit moves away
He goes to seek the crowd
Anywhere loud – towards the light of day.
This striding turmoil
From stolen rest
Requests an answer
So his quest may cease.
And so he walks.

Among the throng
This dour apparition spoors
An uncaring world.

His presence now unnerves the crowd,
The feeling of a walking shroud
Among them
Haunting, flaunting his ghostly cares!
But he didn't hear the whispered talking
He really is a dead man walking.

THE HOTTEST DOG IN TOWN

I get myself all smarted up
To get in with the action.
I ride my motorbike to town
To get myself some traction.

And as I walk into the bar
Where all the females huddle,
I cast my eye around them all
To sort the ones to cuddle.

Then it's up onto the dance floor
Where the handbags all are laid,
And the gals all shimmy up my way
And opportunities cascade!

And then I'm howling like a wolf
And really shaking booty,
And with the girls all joining in
I'm cuddling with a cuty.

And now the place is hotting up
I'm building up a sweat,
And then I have to strip my kit
Cause I'm starting to get wet.

So now I'm sliding up and down
Inside my finger roll,
And getting hotter all the time
With the mustard in control.

KEYS

I listen to the slow approach
And clanking keys of Papa Diddle.
His wincing gasp. This slow coach
Turns the key
The key of night
To take the sunshine from my sight.
He drones away at his creed.

I eye the brass ring full of keys,
The paracentric, abloy, cruciform
And wide jawed skeleton.
"I have to listen to your sermon, but please
Allow me the feel of bitted keys."

The clank and jank of lifted iron
Tantalises my grateful gaze.
His whiskered, cankered closeness
Brushes my face near the dimple key.

"Grant me the key for the Gordian knot
The one that was by you ill got,
To allow me a modicum of phot
To ease my time with you somewhat."

He yields for me a cruciform.
It seems to feel as if a storm
Of shredded time escapes away –
And doesn't need to use a day
To fit its purpose.

JILLIAN

I'm lying here upon my bed
With all this babble in my head.
Who was it that made the decree
That this life should be lived by me?

As a child, my life was great,
As for the future – I couldn't wait.
When the sixties were in full swing
I didn't worry about a thing.

I went to college to get smart,
Like other girls, I lost my heart.
Everyone thought I would go far;
My life was following a lucky star.

But then came the fateful day,
An evil curse had found its way
To paralyse my every move,
When I still had so much to prove.

Then came the doctors thick and fast,
I hoped and prayed it wouldn't last.
But just like an invidious foe,
It brought me down and laid me low.

As time went on, and as it grew
Friends drifted off, to leave those who
Would come and help wipe my backside.
It didn't leave an ounce of pride.

And as the years dragged slowly by,
Nerve damage made me want to die.
No change in faculty to my brain –
Just stopped me moving ever again.

A block of wood has more function.
There never is an introduction
For me to meet somebody new –
They must have better things to do.

I never talk to a single soul
Except to those who come to roll
My broken body – and wash it clean.
A conversation – that's my dream.

But no one comes. This lonely bed
Breeds lots of poison in my head.
I am condemned to go berserk
And see those who treat me as work.

So why is it, my life is so
When I have nothing – no place to go?
You think your life is full of care
But would you have mine and not be there?

HOLIDAY ALL THE WAY

(Based on the Wallace Arnold coach film on 1950's/60's travel)

Jolly Molly gets on the coach
To go on the continent.
Why shouldn't you?
You know it's what you want to do.

To get the air, sky and sea,
We know it's where we want to be.
We waited for it all winter long
And on the coach we sing our songs.

In the highlands we see the deer
And hear the piper piping cheer.
Then we drive by the lochs
And see the sheep in all their flocks.

And then for lunch we're at the inn
To get our pints of beer and din.
Then we join the tour for France.
This lovely country will sure entrance.

Then we're on to Lake Geneva,
I wonder if we'll spot a beaver!
Rocher de Nieux is the place to go
Along the rails in the snow.

Then at the Perle du lac
For our lunch – or just a snack?
After we're on the bench to snooze –
It must have been all that booze!

Then there's peacocks or fish in the pool,
It's just the way to keep us cool
Then up on to the chair lift –
The views are such a lovely gift.

We need to get our souvenirs
'Cause soon we'll be leaving here.
And sort out all these funny coins
And miss blue skies and bubbling sunshine.

CHERRY

My love is like a ripe red cherry,
Pert, squashy and delicious.
Its taste…wraps around my lovers mouth
It fills him with delight
As he samples the deep sweetness
That tingles thought his soul.
My cherry thrills him
Wills him
To come back for more,
And he tastes again and again
Till his senses are filled with
Cherry juice.

BETRAYAL

I see you in the shadows,
In her sweet embrace.
I feel my poor heart breaking;
Could you not tell me to my face?

I watch you holding hands
As you meander down the lane.
I pull myself together
As my senses I regain.

You walk into the darkness
And disappear from sight.
I begin to formulate my plan –
My revenge I will ignite.

Next day I see you share a joke
In a street café.
Then I watch you pay the bill
And see you walk away.

Down the street you window shop
Outside a jeweller's store.
I see her eyes aglitter,
Then you enter through the door.

When you come outside
There's a diamond on her finger.
I see the love upon your face,
And I watch your kisses linger.

I see you walking hand in hand
And bid a fond farewell.
I hear the front door open,
Then I see your Jezabel.

My sister stands in front of me
To flash her shiny ring.
I say that I am happy for her
And she doesn't suspect a thing.

I hear you later on the phone;
I hear her honeyed words.
She thinks she'll get away with this-
I think that she's absurd.

"You know you took him from me,
He was my only man.
It was always in your wicked head-
Your gross and evil plan."

"So don't you ever think that
I'll let you make him yours,
The time now has come for me
To even up the scores."

I raise my right arm quickly
To strike her on the head.
But she brings the knife up squarely
And cuts at me instead.

My blood flows red and pure-
And seems to fill the room.
And with her glittering diamond
Your love is free to bloom.

SACHA AND THE BLOW UP DOG

My owners have a blow up doll –
They use it every night.
It really seems to cheer them up
Each morning smiles are bright.

I'd really like to have someone
To cheer my night time too.
I really am a lonely dog
And sometimes I get blue.

And so I set upon my quest
To make a plastic friend.
I need some rubber tubing,
Floppy, so it'll bend.

I know there are black dustbin bags
Hidden somewhere on the shelf.
I'll stick them round with sellotape
Then blow it up myself.

I carefully cut the rubber tube
And make it into legs,
Then bend the plastic body
For it to sit up and beg.

The only thing that's missing now,
It doesn't have a head.
There's a ventriloquist's dummy
Beneath my master's bed.

It looks a bit of an oddity
With the head of Kermit Frog,
I'd rather hoped to finish it
So it looks more like a dog.

But never mind, it does just fine
I won't be lonely now,
He's my friend for cuddling close
If that's what he'll allow.

HOLLY

It had left a trail
And been hot and passionate
When it had been generously given from my heart.
Venom had been exchanged
And words so fickle
Like shards of glass –
They broke and pierced me.
And so it trailed
And imprinted my skin
With a sticky red edged line –
The pain an exhibit for all to see.
Now December infiltrates the world
And a bossy tree with berries
Stands proud and mocking
Ready to spike my injured soul.
Blood filled berries
Fill the boughs,
And my tears hang heavy
With the holly.

FANTASY

We ride the rainbow –
Slide down the rainbow,
To the pool of gold.
Fantasies of mist
By angels we are kissed,
And all our dreams unfold.

We're floating around
In kaleidoscopic hues.
While we gaze at the trees so green.
And showers of stars
We collect in our jars,
While spirits look on unseen.

Dewdrops sparkle like diamonds
Scattered around our feet.
Clouds of pearl and pink.
Petals fall from the sky
And a fairy drifts by,
In a marshmallow world we sink.

Butterflies flutter by
In a flurry of gentle breeze.
We hear hummingbirds call,
Their voices find truths
For our hearts to be soothed,
And sorrow from the world must fall.

SOMEWHERE

After we had had our talk,
I took our dog out for a walk.
You said that we should see a show –
But then we weren't sure where to go.
I walked the woods and heard a noise,
I thought it was just rowdy boys.
But then I ran behind a thicket,
Peeped round - and saw a speeding ticket
In the wind - flying round and round
Then it dropped down to the ground.

It was for a magic carpet ride,
To go to the land of Whitsuntide.
A sunny place - away and distant,
Somewhere so we may recant
Deeds and thoughts we know were wrong,
So we may sing a different song.
And live somewhere, not in this 'now',
But somewhere else to show us how
Things may have been, if we had known
And not have made this world our home.

I eyed the bill, thought long and deep
Could I allow another world to creep
Into my life, and make a change
Where everything I knew was strange?

I tore the ticket and went on my way,
To make the most of this lovely day.

FOREVER

Volcanic respiratory explosion abound,
As he heaves his gait to the edge of the bed-
Disturbing my sleep. I open my eyes
And watch his silhouette as he sits close by.
I reach out
And gather warmth from his frame.
He searches urgently for my hand
To squeeze and reassure.

Then he lies near me
And wraps me securely in his arms.
Finding my lips, his kisses
Are warm and reciprocated.

I gaze into his face
And he says the words I am about to say,
Of undying love
Of unimaginable depths
Of love everlasting.
Impenetrable-
And wonderfully selfish.

He rises up
Tucks me underneath
And kisses me
With exultations
Of passions and pleasures
To keep forever.

We reluctantly draw apart
To participate again and again
While inside we grow wild and wilder
Each grasping the others desire
To fulfil and create more passions.

Each wonders, incredulously-
At the others power,
To engender the feelings
That pass between us.
At the waves of magic,
That bind us inextricably,
Forever.

Printed in Great Britain
by Amazon

12173711R00058